# Religion & Science

*Thoughts of a Common Jim*

James Hillman

WESTBOW
PRESS®
A DIVISION OF THOMAS NELSON
& ZONDERVAN

WestBow Press books may be ordered through booksellers or by contacting:

WestBow Press
A Division of Thomas Nelson & Zondervan
1663 Liberty Drive
Bloomington, IN 47403
www.westbowpress.com
1 (866) 928-1240

Taken from the HOLY BIBLE: EASY-TO-READ VERSION © 2001 by
World Bible Translation Center, Inc. and used by permission.

ISBN: 978-1-9736-6843-5 (sc)
ISBN: 978-1-9736-6842-8 (e)

Print information available on the last page.

WestBow Press rev. date: 07/16/2019

This book is dedicated to

Tina my Wife, my Love, and my anchor
My parents for all of the help that they've given us
To all my friends and to the strangers whose questions and comments inspired this book
Thank you all

# Contents

# My Faith Views

❖

This is my Faith on paper. The limits of this paper are defined by my ability to communicate what is in my heart.

To help understand my point-of-view, you need to understand that I am a big reader of history. I don't just read the dry facts of "So-and-so did such-and-such on this date-in-time at this-location." I go looking for "Why" and "How" it happened. When I read history, I do my best to "See" the events as if I were truly there.

I also try to see both sides of any issue that I encounter. I have noticed over the years that most people only want to see their own side of a given issue. On the down side, this does cause me to be a slow debater. But, on the up side, it allows me to get a more complete picture.

I do not question scripture itself, but, I do question the interpretation and usage of scripture. A good example; many talk about how the husband has dominion over his wife as in the $1^{st}$ half of 1 Corinthians 7:4, but overlook the $2^{nd}$ half, where it says that the wife will also have dominion over the husband.

# Who am I and why did I write this?

❖

I am not the scholar or the scientist or the theologian that stands behind the podium. I am the one sitting in the crowd watching and listening to the one behind the podium.

I am a retired Army sergeant with 20 years of service and a veteran of Desert Storm (Combat Air Brigade of 3rd Armored Division). I would have to say that I was an average solder. I have a Bachelor's degree in computers. I have worked for the Mississippi Department Of Transportation for over 17 years. I've read much about religion and science, but I'm not a scientist or theologian.

I have many friends that are not Christian. They've had many questions about my religion and my faith. Over the years, I've tried to answer their questions to the best of my ability. I also found myself answering the same type of questions from friends who are Christians. In time, I started to write down these questions and my answers in an effort to find better explanations to answer their questions.

From these discussions, came this book.

My answers came from what I have been taught, from what I have read from various sources, and from my own observations. My answers came also from my walk through life with GOD. As with any walk in life, there are many stops and milestones along the way.

As a child, I was taught that GOD sees us for who we are. But all of the grownups were putting a very high emphasis on a person's outward appearance as if you had to wear a suit and tie in order to show your purity. There were also a lot of arguing about which denomination was closer to GOD and which one was nowhere near to GOD.

From time to time, there were incidents that raised red flags in my mind. One such was the song "Luka" by Suzanna Vega which brought attention to child abuse and encouraged people to try their best to stop it from happening. Many of the Church elders of the day blasted the song for talking about it because child abuse was something that shouldn't have been talked about. Their reaction to this song confused me. I mean, here they were searching out sin to expose it, but, when the sin of child abuse is mentioned, they acted as if they were personally insulted. Another song that was blasted in a similar way was "Only Women Bleed" by Alice Cooper. This song spoke of spouse abuse with the same goal of bringing it to an end, but, the song was also attacked in the same way for the same reasons.

I had always been a big reader as far back as I can remember. I had read and was starting to memorize all of the <u>Hardy Boys</u> books that had been published up to 6<sup>th</sup> grade which was about a hundred by that time, not to mention who knows how many dinosaur books. As I read though the books on Western history, I learned of the many wars of religion that Christians inflicted on each other. I also learned of how Christians treated Native Americans, Africans, and Asians. I also saw how the rich often treated the lower classes. On the news, I saw many of the same things were still going on in one form or another.

By this time, I was starting to have many doubts about the Church. If there was any way to sum up my thoughts in music, it would be the songs "Sunday Bloody Sunday" by U2, "Give Me Something to Believe In" by Poison, and "Rose Colored Stained Glass Windows" by Petra. The thing that still amazes me to this day is that I never questioned GOD or Scripture.

Everything came to a head in April of '91. Desert Storm was over. We had moved from the desert of Southern Iraq to a bombed out army base in Northern Kuwait. I was listening to the radio, a preacher was giving a sermon. I don't remember most of the sermon but I do remember that he was talking about the recent war with Iraq. In it, he called the war itself Glorious, Noble, and Beautiful.

Now to me, the liberation of Kuwait was indeed Glorious and Noble and most definitely should have been done, I'm glad that I was a part of it, but, there is nothing glorious, noble, or beautiful about war itself. It is an evil necessity of last resort when all else fails. But there was a definite arrogance in his tone. It was if we (the US) was "Bringing the Light of Civilization" to this part of the world. For those of you who don't know "Bringing the Light of Civilization to the world" was the reason/excuse for Western Imperialism.

At this point, I said "GOD, my faith in you is absolute. However, I no longer have any faith in the Church." Even though I continued to pray and study the Bible, it was a few years before I could set foot in a church building, and many years before doing any formal worship at a church.

There are those who will question my ability to walk with GOD without the help of a congregation. In fact, I was asked how it could be done. My answer was "It ain't easy."

The best way to describe this is by using an analogy. Let's say that the Bible is a roadmap, the congregation is a car (or any form of transportation), and the road of life is a road going from say New York to L.A. Going from New York to L.A. with a car is infinitely easier than going by foot but as long as you have your roadmap, it can be done. However, going by foot allows you to see things that you would never have seen going by car.

In the same way, I learned many things about the world that I hadn't seen before. Mostly, how many non-believers see GOD and the Church.

I'm not saying that I made an easy choice of how I chose to walk with GOD or that it was a "Good" or "Right" choice. I know that I had a reason for it.

# Laws of Nature and Scripture

To start, I will state three things;

1.   Religion is the current understanding and usage of Scripture.
2.   Science is the current understanding and usage of the Laws of Nature.
3.   To me, the Laws of Nature and Scripture are two sides of the same coin.

The last one might need some explaining. The 1ˢᵗ song that I can remember singing was "He has the whole World in His hands." For those of you who are unfamiliar with the song, it talks about how God holds everything from the world as a whole, to the stars in the sky, down to the tiniest raindrop. When I learned this song, I was able to picture God holding everything described in the song, and to be honest, I didn't think much about it. As time went by, I learned about the solar system and molecules, and I could see Him holding both in His hands and again, I didn't think much about it. As more time past, I learned about galaxies, the universe, atoms and subatomic particles, and as I learned about them, I could still picture God holding them in His hands, but still I didn't think much about it.

Then came that fateful day in 1999. In the fall of 1999, I saw a documentary about the String Theory. In it, they talked about quantum particles, quantum physics, and the M-theory: which states that there are multiple universes and that our universe is just one of many. At this point, I could picture God holding a quantum particle and the multiverse at the same time. Something clicked. God had made both of them! God wrote the Laws of Science! Science is the explanation of the physical world that God has created!

I am not the first person to come up with this thought, not by a long shot. In fact, this was the prevailing view for many scientists for most of history. As I understand it, many scientists have come to God, not through scripture, but through science itself.

# Mysteries and Contradictions

There is one constant when looking at Religion vs. Science debates. When it comes to talking about the unknowns, the things/topics that currently have no explanations, within their own arguments, both sides call these unknowns mysteries, and call the unknowns in the other's arguments contradictions or worse. In short they are both saying "It's ok if there is something that can't be explained in our argument because it's simply a mystery waiting to be answered. But the unexplained in your argument is, of course, either a contradiction or something completely made up."

One example is the issue of planetary formation. According to detractors of the Nebular Hypothesis, there are at least two dozen different issues/problems with this hypothesis. This list of issues/problems goes beyond the scope of this book, but religious detractors uses this list to prove that the hypothesis is not just disproven but a work of fiction. Scientist counter-fire by saying that the Nebular Hypothesis best fits the data, and, that yes there is still much to learn.

On the other side of the Nebular Hypothesis is the Church's answer which is; GOD made it.

Let's take a look at this answer with an analogy. Picture yourself at a party and you've come across a marvelous dish, a dish so good that you absolutely have to have the recipe. To get it, you ask your friend, Clara, and the two of you have the following conversation;

You: "Who made this?"

Clara: "Sandra made it."

You: "Is she still here?"

Clara: "No she had to leave."

You: "Do you know if she used any eggs?"

Clara: "Sandra made it."

You: "I know that but do you know if she used any eggs?"

Clara: "Sandra made it."

You: "If you don't know, please just say so."

Clara: angrily "What part of 'Sandra made it' do you not understand?"

Scientist don't mind if holes are poked into their theories as long as that someone can give a better explanation. However "GOD did it" may explain the "Who" but does nothing to explain the "How." To be honest, while I do believe that GOD made the solar system I too would love to know how HE did it.

Another issue concerns many of the stories in the Old Testament. Many historians and archaeologist dismiss them as copies of stories from other traditions in the region. The reason that they do so is because these other traditions were written during a time that the Hebrew faith was still an oral tradition.

Historians and archaeologist dismiss oral traditions saying that only written ones are "truthful" or "faithful" and therefore valid. Theologians and representatives of various cultures have counter-fired by saying that historians and archaeologist are ignoring history because it doesn't fit an excepted view of history or that gathering oral traditions and histories would be too messy or problematic.

When I look at the two sides of these and similar issues I see two groups of people who are so deeply entrenched in their minds that they have to be right, that they have to hear the other side "you're right and I was wrong" that they can't hear what the other side is actually saying. Both seem to be saying "I'm right so why should I listen to you?" To make things worse, there are those on both sides that mock the other side for being "wrong."

To me this is bad science, bad theology, and just plain bad behavior.

# Language Barriers

❖

Another problem with the Science vs Religion debates is the language barrier. I'm not talking about English or French type language but in the way that people think.

For example; to many people around the world chocolate milk is a combination of milk and chocolate that is mixed in the correct amounts. However to the scientific minded it's more like; $C_6H_{12}O_6$ + $C_{12}H_{22}O_6$ + (well hopefully you get the idea). Scientific minded people tend to see things in terms of chemistry, physics, and math. The religious minded sees chocolate milk as: GOD's Blessing of milk with GOD's Blessing of chocolate. The religious minds sees thing in terms of what GOD has given us.

In order for there to be true dialog between the two sides, the two have to learn how to speak the others language. Why? Let's look at an analogy.

Let's say that you know someone who doesn't know any language that you speak and you don't know his language nor have either of you tried to do so. Now, imagine that you're in a room with a window to the room next to it. The widow doesn't have glass, but instead it has a screen. You see that there is a table in that room, on that table is a glass of clear liquid. This liquid may look like water, but for whatever reason, you known, that the clear liquid is actually cyanide. Then you see this person come in and you can see that he is very thirsty, thirsty enough to go straight for what looks to him to be a glass of water. Now if he drinks from that glass, he will die and you are the only person that can save him, but you can only do it by speaking to him.

Now here's the question. How do you save this person's life without being able to speak his language? The answer; you can't.

More than once I've heard scientific minded persons speak of saving the religious from their ignorance of how the world actually works. The thing is until you can translate science into theology, you can't.

More than once, I've heard various religious leaders speak of saving the scientific minded persons from their lack of faith and belief. The thing is, until you can translate theology into science, you can't.

# Greatest myth ever

❖

To atheist the greatest myth ever, would have to be religion. To many Christians, it would have to be either atheism or polytheism. To many spiritualists, it would be that spirits don't exist. I'm positive that Buddhist and Confucianist would have their say in the matter as well. One thing that all of the above have in common is that to each "the greatest myth ever is the one that disagrees with what I believe."

I would have to say that there is one bigger muth. This myth has been around for thousands of years and existed around the world long before the first trade routes were ever established. This myth is "we already know everything that there is to know."

Jared Diamond wrote a book called <u>Collapse</u>. In his book, he gave a number of reasons that a civilization can collapse. He is not the first to do so. There have been a number of historians who have weighed in this subject. In his book Diamond talked about how "we already know everything that there is to know" has weakened and ended a number of civilizations.

To me it seems that the myth of "we already know everything that there is to know" has most likely contributed greatly of the collapse of almost any civilization that you care to mention.

# How much do we know?

How much do we know about the universe and its laws? If we were to use education levels as an analogy, then we could say that having absolute knowledge of the universe and its laws would be equal to having a doctorates degree. Where does humanities' knowledge of the universe fall on this scale? I would say probably 1st grade. In other words, there is just way too much that we just don't know. Why do I say this? Look at how often humanity has said "This thing is impossible" only to have Mother Nature prove us wrong.

# The Impossible

How do we know what is possible or impossible? Think about it. Prior to the locomotive, logic dictated that man could not travel faster than 45mph. If he did, the air would rush past his mouth so fast he could not breathe, he would suffocate and die. Prior to the submarine, the idea that a ship could sink itself and then resurface on its own, deliberately, was ludicrous. The idea that you could have a material that when heated acted like wax but when cool acted like iron (i.e. plastic), would have landed you in the loony bin.

Shortly after the Guttenberg press was invented, a nobleman bought 6 copies of the Bible printed by the press and took them to Paris. When he showed them to his friends, they burned the books as works of the Devil. They felt that the only way to make 6 perfect copies of any book was by using black magic.

The point that I'm trying to make is, every bit of technology that is in your life that you take for granted, at some point in the past, was considered totally and logically impossible. The boundary between what is possible and impossible is defined by current technology.

Just because it is impossible today, does not mean that it will be impossible tomorrow.

So what does this mean about GOD?

To me it means that GOD uses Laws of Nature that Humanity has yet to discover.

# Where is the Scientific Proof for God

Before I get into this one, I would like to point out that most scientist don't like to get involved in any kind of Religious/Science debate mainly because it is often heavily charged with emotions. When they do allow themselves to get into such a debate with one person, often another person will ask "But what about My god?"

One possibility of where to find scientific evidence for GOD is that science is hiding or suppressing the evidence that GOD is real. That might work in Hollywood but not in the real world. THERE IS NO SINGULAR PIECE OF EVIDENCE THAT GOD IS REAL THAT CAN BE LOST OR HIDDEN OR DESTROYED LIKE IN A HOLLYWOOD DRAMA. Instead, it is more like losing, hiding, or destroying the evidence that the Earth goes around the Sun instead of the other way around.

In John 3:8, it says, although you can't see the wind, you can hear the wind acting on the leaves. In a way it reminds me of discussions of Dark Matter and Dark Energy. Dark Matter is matter that we cannot detect with any of our five senses or current technology. The same is true of Dark Energy. While neither one be detected by any of our current technology there is much indirect evidence that they do exist.

I believe that the most likely evidence for GOD will be in the same way as Dark Matter, not direct but indirect.

Another possibility is that the right technology needed to get the evidence has not been invented.

For a long time, there has been the theory that there might possibly be planets orbiting other suns. For a long time, the theory remained in the world of Science Fiction. Then the telescopes got better. They got better through the use of a number of breakthroughs in astronomy technology and better ideas in using the new technology. Then they found the 1ˢᵗ planet outside of our own solar system.

Now we know that most, if not all suns, have at least one or two planets of their own.

We may already have the proof that GOD is real, but, we might not see it for what it is. Impossible? Not quite.

As I understand it, one night, an astronomer was making observations of some stars and saw one star go dark. With the advent of aviation and satellites, this does happen from time to time. For this reason, most astronomers have charts that tell them of airline and satellite paths and their flight times. When this happened, he looked at his charts and found the sky was clear at that time. He noted the event in his notes and went back to his work. After a time, the star came back; he made a note of that as well. After some more time passed, he sees another star go dark. This really got his attention. He made another note and waited for the star to return. When it did, he made a note of that. He noted the time that the two stars had been dark and noticed that they were the same. He calculated the time between the stars going dark, drew a line between the two, and extended the line to the next star. He calculated that if this phenomenon was going to happen again, it would happen to that star at a given time. At that given time the said star did go dark for the same amount of time. The phenomenon happened exactly as he calculated.

He sent out this finding and asked if any others had come across the same thing. Across the world, archived observations were checked. It turns out that such observations had been made since the invention of the telescope. These observations became the first evidence that Black Holes are real. Much in the same way, it is very possible that such evidence for GOD has been found but no one has interpreted the evidence correctly.

Another possibility is the misunderstanding of data or information that we already have. How? Simple, through the use of Human Logic. Don't believe me? Ever heard of the Tyrannosaurus Rex?

When the T-Rex was first found, it was unmistakably biped. When they put the bones together to made a complete skeleton, they decided to put it together standing like a human being with the tail bending at an almost 90° angle halfway down and dragging the ground, Human Logic said that was the ONLY way it could stand.

Over time younger paleontologists took note of the kangaroo and similar animals and said "Hold on, there might be another possibility." They swept aside Human Logic, took a closer look at the bones, and found out that it would have been impossible for the T-Rex to stand that way. They followed the evidence, instead of Human Logic, and figured out how the T-Rex really stood up.

We all seek the truth. However, if the truth lies outside of our comfort zone, people tend to either overlook it or fudge it a little so it can be more "palatable." Most of the time we do this subconsciously.

In high school and college, I was told many times, for a scientist, one of their "Commandments" is to "Seek the truth by following the evidence without preconceptions to wherever to it goes and do not allow politics, religion, or culture to bar or influence the way." Scientist, however, are people, and when they encounter evidence that makes them uncomfortable, or, if the path starts taking them in direction that may be political or religious in nature, many may subconsciously edge away from it. A minority, however, would flat-out reject it.

A case in point. A person goes to the doctor and is told that they have incurable cancer. The person then has a religious experience. Later, the person goes back to the doctor who then proclaims that the cancer is in remission or is gone totally. This has happened more than a few times. In fact, this has been documented often enough that the scientific community has had to comment on it. The comment so far that I've heard has been, "It's either divine intervention or placebo" and then they wash their hands of it.

Who cares if it is divine intervention or a placebo! The cure for cancer, very possibly, is right there in front of you. The scientific community has an obligation to follow the evidence, find out what is happening, and figure out a way to trigger it! If it turns out that the cure for cancer is a placebo, so what! You've found the cure for cancer! If it turns out that the cure for cancer is divine intervention, so what! You've still found the cure for cancer!

At this point I can hear some in the Church getting a bit upset with me, saying that GOD wouldn't reveal HIMSELF like that. My reply is that, according to scripture, GOD does reveal HIMSELF through nature (Roman 1:19-20). Also in order for a person to learn something (like how to read) he has to learn the basics (like learning the alphabet, spelling, and basic grammar) to read. It is very possible that GOD wanted us to learn more about the universe through science as a way of revealing more about HIMSELF.

I've actually heard from more than one non-believer that if a religion, any religion, was proven true, that it would be the end of science. I disagree, because many like myself, would turn to scientist and ask "How did these miraculous events happen, what is the science behind them?" To me, discovering that GOD is real would open a door to a brand new field(s) of science.

Another point that I want to make is that a lot of data about nature is collected every year. It takes time to process data into information. It also takes time to turn information into theory. And yes, it takes time to turn theory into technology that can then be used. It's not impossible that we may have already collected the key data needed for Faster-Than-Light travel without anyone knowing about it. In the same way we may already have the key data needed to prove the GOD is real without anyone knowing about.

What we have to remember is that scientists are exploring the unknown. While exploring the unknown, it is very possible that scientists can be wrong about the information that they are looking at. What I would like to point out here is that we all can make mistakes. The Bible tells us to forgive others of their mistakes. If we don't forgive but continue to abuse scientist for their past mistakes that they have admitted to and corrected, then what has happened, and will continue to happen, is more of them turning away from GOD instead of turn to GOD.

# Science: Theory vs. Practical

Many people tend to not see a difference between Practical Science and Theoretical Science.

Practical Science deals with things that are directly part of everyday life. It deals with What Is. Engineering and construction, clinical and hospital medicine, agriculture, mining, and manufacturing are all examples of Practical Science.

Theoretical Science deals with things that are directly or indirectly part of everyday life but is not fully understood. Paleontology and Cosmology are examples of Theoretical Science.

Meteorology and Social Sciences are different in that they are a little of both Practical Science and Theoretical Science.

What needs to be understood is that Practical Science changes very slowly. Theoretical Science changes often because it is the exploration of the unknown. The theories that theoretical scientist put forth are done to the best of their knowledge based on current evidence from their point of view. When their theories change, it is because they have uncovered something new. For some branches, this can happen on a daily bases while for others change happens only once every few decades.

Does this mean that we should disregard all Theoretical Science? No, because most Practical Science STARTED OUT as Theoretical Science.

# Creation/Evolution

I have pondered the best way to describe my views on Creation/Evolution. The best way that I can think of is to start with an analogy.

Picture two people sitting down at a table, between them is a pile of jigsaw pieces.

The 1st person starts putting together some of these pieces. The ones he chooses are 1" square, made of wood, and are painted with water based paint.

The 2nd person also starts putting together some of the other pieces. The ones he chooses are ½" square, made of metal, and are painted with oil based paint.

After a time, the 1st person puts together a picture of two poor people facing to the left of the picture. The problem is that while the top, bottom, and right sides of the puzzle are completed, the left side is incomplete and he has run out of puzzle pieces. The 2nd person, meanwhile, has put together a picture of three rich people looking to the right. His problem is that his picture is complete on all sides but the right and he has also run out of pieces.

The two then begin arguing over who's picture is the most complete.

After a time, one of them looks at the remaining puzzle pieces on the table. He had seen them before but had disregarded them because they were made of stone and were ¾" in size. Now that he is examining them, he notices that some are oil based painted and some are water based painted and some seem to be a little of both. He then starts to put them together. The other person, at some point, joins in.

When they are done, they find that only the top and bottom is complete while the sides are still incomplete. They also notice that the left side is oil painted and the right is water painted with the middle having the oil and water paints joining in such a way as to complement each other. The picture is of an infant wrapped in cloth lying in a wooden box filled with what looks like straw or hay. The truly odd part is that the left side is fitted to mate with ½" pieces and the right side is fitted to mate with 1" pieces.

After looking at the three puzzles, they first fix the wooden picture to the stone one and then they fit the metal picture to the stone one. After doing so, they saw a complete picture of a manger scene.

The metal and wood represent creation and evolution facts and theories. The stone represents the missing data that, when found, will bridge and connect the other two.

What are those missing pieces? I haven't a clue.

These missing pieces might be sitting right in front of us. They might be waiting for us to make some kind of technological breakthrough. Why did God chose to do it this way? I don't know, I only know that he has.

So what does this say about Genesis 1? To me, Genesis 1 is a 200 word summery of a 2 million word scientific document written in a way that anyone no matter their age, educational, philosophical, theological, or cultural background can read and understand it.

There are many who would say that even so, the Bible is still a complete scientific document. I disagree and here's why.

Let's look at Genesis 1:3 "Then God said 'Let there be light!' and then there was light." In order for Genesis 1:3 to be scientifically accurate it would need to say "Then God said 'Let there be light! *and then using (list of elements used, list of energies used, list of Laws of Nature used, list of processes used) He then (sequence of events with descriptions of where, when, how, and why of the creation of light)* and then there was light."

Of course if the Bible was written this way, each passage of each miraculous event would end up being a complete book in its own right!

# Commandments, Virtues, and Sins

❖

God has many rules. Why does He have them? The simplest answer is twofold.

First: He places these rules to let us know the best way to create a better world for everyone. If you look at many of His rules without any religious context you will see that the underlying context has been seen around the world in many forms. Why? Because they are based on logic not emotion or a desire to control. Surprised? Many of the rules are for sanitation and health like the Kosher rules for what foods to eat and not to eat. Others are for how to treat each other without hurting or offending the other person.

Second: He places these rules to determine who He is going to let into His home which is Heaven. We all do this in form or another. Think about it, would you invite someone into your home that would not respect your property? Of course not! The same is true for Him.

Alright let's see if we can look at them through the eyes of Logic instead of Religion.

## *Commandments*

1. <u>Do not have any other god before God</u>. In Matthew 6:24 it says "You cannot serve two masters for you will love one and hate the other, or you will be loyal to one and not care about the other."

I think that we've all seen this one. A person has two jobs and from time to time there is a schedule conflict. Each time this happens the person will all ways pick either one or the other.

History has shown that most of the strongest people in the world are those who hold to having a power that is greater than themselves. Be it a religion, a political ideology, their follow man or what have you. There is something that happens when a person gives themselves to a higher cause and it has been noticed and commented on by countless historians, philosophers, sociologist, and phycologist.

This greater power is your master. This is your guiding light, your inspiration, and sometimes it's your reason to just get out of bed every morning. However, just like in the job conflict above you can't have two of them. Eventually you'll end up having to choose between them.

2.   Do not make yourself an idol.

This is tied in with the First Commandment. An idol is at its simplest a false greater power. This false greater power can be many different things but most often it's one's own arrogance. It's worshiping yourself, it's seeing yourself as infallible as if you can somehow make the world as you want it to be.

Perhaps the most well-known example of this would be Adolf Hitler. He believed that through his own force of will that he could make Nazi Germany the greatest power on earth capable of doing anything and beating anyone or any nation that he chose to take on.

Other false greater powers do have power of their own. These powers are; money, politics, law, lawlessness, popularity, lust, technology, hate, fear, desperation, and despair just to name a few. This form of false power is anything that gives you the power to control someone else or has power over you.

So how does one know the difference between God and one of these false powers? To me God gives guidance not dominance or domination. It's not about being controlled or controlling others. It's also not about giving up the material as it is about not being controlled by the material. It's also about receiving and not taking from others.

Yep, it sounds like mystical nonsense doesn't it? That's because it's not always easy to explain. In fact a good part of the Bible is about explaining this mystical nonsense and there are many books out there that go into this from many different viewpoints.

There many other types of false gods which I'll be going over in the section **Personalities.**

3.   Do not take the Lord's name in vain.

As I understand it, in ancient times this commandment meant pledging an oath to God and then going back on it. Now I'm not talking about in a general sense but as something very specific as in "I pledge to go to this city and start converting people to your name." If you make this pledge and try and fail from God's view you can and will be forgiven but if you make the pledge and never try that is a very different story. That is taking the Lord's name in vain.

4.   Remember the Sabbath Day and keep it holy.

When the Bible goes into detail about what this means, it says, that on the Sabbath you stop all work and reflect on your own life and God's impact on it. This makes a lot of sense when you think about it. According to sociologist and phycologist all people have a breaking point. When you work beyond that point, your ability to work takes a hit. You start getting sloppy and careless. In time you can end up hurting yourself or someone else in some form or another. You actually have to stop working from time to time and take a break.

Also according to many phycologist and philosophers taking time to reflect on your life is a very good idea. It's a lot like navigating from one point to another. Have you ever driven somewhere and missed a turn because you weren't paying attention? That is exactly what this commandment is talking about. Stopping, taking a look around to see where you are, looking to where you want to be, figuring out if you're on course or not, and then making any changes needed to stay or to get back on course.

5. <u>Honor thy Mother and Father (Elders)</u>.

There was a point where Bill Cosby said that he and his wife had Doctor's Degrees in child phycology which meant that that were over qualified to be parents. When they had their first child, they found out just how little that they knew which was pretty close to nothing. Their parents could have told them that one.

When I was in the Army, we had a term called "Subject Matter Experts" or SME for short. Mostly, these were people who learned by doing, not only did they understand their subject but they KNEW it.

Your parents have lived through more than you have which makes them an SME in many subjects.

Yes, there are many who have parents that are not good role models. I'll be honest, mine are good role models and this makes it very difficult to understand and connect to those who don't have such parents.

6. <u>Do not murder</u>.

This is one and the next three tends to be some of first laws that any community creates. I'm sure that there are some plenty of lengthy explanations out there from sociologist and historians but for our purposes here I'm going to keep things simple. These four commandments help to create trust between people.

If people know that you are not known to harm others they will reach out to you to create bonds of business and friendship which are the foundation of all communities and it is communities that form nations.

7. <u>Do not commit adultery</u>.

Marriage is a bond that is held above all others in many cultures, religions, and traditions. It is a UNION that is held above all others. In ancient times to almost recent times when two kingdoms form an alliance the sealing act of the alliance would be a marriage between two of their important persons. The tradition of arranged marriages has often been defended by saying that marriage is too important for emotions to get involved. In modern times, I often hear of two corporations' merger as a marriage.

Marriage is seen as a melding of two lives into one shared life. It is the greatest of unions. Therefore if a person is willing to treat the marriage as something less than a true bonding then all other oaths are suddenly in question.

8. <u>Do not steal</u>.

One day someone came onto our property and stole our lawnmower. When I saw that it was missing, I felt violated. I was more than upset, I was angry. I'll admit that the idea of hurting the person or persons involved was very tempting.

This is often how wars, family arguments, and divorces occur. It is the idea that the other person has stolen something from them. Stealing creates the idea that the other person cannot be trusted, not now, not ever.

9. <u>Do not testify false witness against your neighbor</u>.

Lying is often seen as an attack on someone. It's attacking their name, their character. It's about attacking who they are.

Now let me clarify something right now. Lying is about KNOWING that what you are saying is not correct and yet still saying it as if it were the truth. That is not the same as saying something that you know to be true but is actually incorrect. If someone tells you a falsehood and convinces you that they are tell you the truth and you then go and tell someone else then you yourself are not lying. Once you find out the truth but you continue to tell the falsehood then you are lying.

10. <u>Do not covet</u>.

To me this one has got to be the most important of the commandments because it is about thoughts. Coveting is about thinking about possessing what someone else has. It's not about saying "Hey, I'd love to have a house/car/job/wife like or similar what he has." It's about saying "Hey, I'd love to have the house/car/job/wife that he has."

Just about any phycologist can tell you that ALL action starts with thought. You cannot stand up without first thinking "I want to stand up." We might not think of the individual steeps, of flexing the back and leg muscles needed to stand up, but we do think of the desire and the pursuit of said desire to stand up.

It's all about mindset. If you have the mindset to obey the local driving laws, then you'll not be speeding or running red lights/stop signs or any other actions that tend to make cops upset.

Even though it's the last of the commandments it all starts here.


*Virtues*

There is no one list of Seven Virtues, not even within the Church itself. The list that I am using was defined by Pope Gregory.

1.  <u>Faith</u> is belief in the right things (including the virtues themselves!).

How does one explain Faith? It's more than just believing in something or someone. To me, it is believing in something or someone even when Human Logic starts to fail. It is about facing difficult times and knowing you will get through it. It is about facing the unknown and knowing that it's ok even if you don't get all of the answers. I've heard others explain it in similar ways. For many people that I've spoken to over the years, this explanation doesn't quite cut it and I've struggled to come up with a better way to explain it.

Then one day I overheard two women talking. One was very late in her pregnancy and the other turned out to have had at least one child of her own. As I listened to their conversation they talked about the aches and pains of being pregnant. Listening to their words, the words themselves sounded very general and vague but looking at their facial expressions and body language and hearing their tone of their voices I could tell that they were being very specific and detailed, but the only way to understand them would be to have experienced being pregnant yourself.

For those of you, who find my explanations of Faith a bit vague, please don't overlook my descriptions, for they'll help to recognize Faith when you finally find it.

2.  <u>Hope</u> is taking a positive future view, that something good can and will prevail.

Hope is Faith's companion and works much the same way. In many ways it's even harder to explain. Faith is the believing in something while Hope is the believing in the POSSIBILITY of something.

3.  <u>Charity</u> is concern for, and active helping of, others.

There is more to Charity then giving money or time to a worthy cause. Let me ask you this. Why does the Coast Guardsman sail into the teeth of a raging storm? Why does a firefighter charge into the inferno of a burning building? Why does a police officer race to the sound of gunfire? Is it money? Trust me they don't get paid that much. Is it fame? What fame they get, often ends before the news-show is over. The reason they do this is the Virtue of Charity.

4.  <u>Fortitude</u> is never giving up.

This means never giving up even when Human Logic says it's Game Over. Fortitude is what gives Faith and Hope they muscle that they need. At the same time Faith and Hope is what gives Fortitude life. I know I'm setting a "Chicken and Egg" argument but with the human mind a tiny spark of one will lead to igniting the second which will set the first on fire and then the two will grow together.

5.  <u>Justice</u> is being fair and equitable with others.

Vengeance is the anti-mater of Justice. Justice knows when it is time for the punishment has been done and time for it to end. However, Vengeance is not satisfied with punishing the guilty for that crime but to smash the guilty beyond their crime and perhaps to others that might have been involved.

As long as there is pain or even the memory of pain the desire for Vengeance will always be there. However, Justice allows for Forgiveness (see Forgiving Others below).

6.  <u>Prudence</u> is care of and moderation with money.

To the Virtue of Prudence money is not a possession but a resource to be used wisely and skillfully. There is a very thin line between Prudence and Greed and sometimes it's hard to tell the difference.

To me the difference between the two is that Prudence will give up money when it is needed but Greed will not.

7.  <u>Temperance</u> is moderation of needed things and abstinence from things which are not needed.

Temperance understands that the phrase "you can't have too much of a good thing" is not always true. For example you need vitamin D to live, if you don't have enough vitamin D you'll a have a number of health issues. However if you take in too much vitamin D you'll get sick.


*Sins*

Interestingly there is very little variation in this list within the Church and most of that is in the order in which they are placed. The History Channel did a series on the Seven Sins called "Seven Deadly Sins." In this series they talked about the history of this list, where the individual sins can be found in the Bible, what others religions say about each individual sin, and modern evidence for each individual sin. There is absolutely no way I can top their findings but I will give you some personal thoughts on each.

1.  <u>Pride</u>

"Pride goeth before a fall." Proverbs 16:18. To my understanding, most if not all religions have this saying in one form or another and it is easy to see why. There are beyond countless numbers of examples throughout the world and throughout history of someone self-declaring that they can do no wrong only to fall flat on their face.

Pride is also at the root of all of the other sins. Because a person says "Yes, bad things have happened to others who follow that road, but, those bad things can't possibly happen to me."

2.  <u>Envy</u>

This is where the Deadly Sins starts to reach out and drives the person by filling the person's mind with "I Want, I want, I Want." It is the thought process of "What I have is not good enough because someone else has something better." It is about not being happy with their F-250 truck because someone else has an F-350 truck, or not being happy with their sports car because someone else has a faster one.

The person becomes blind to all else. A person's world could be falling apart but they won't notice until they think that their envy is satisfied. The person could also be blind to the reality of what or who they want, that what they are seeing could be nothing more than an illusion.

## 3. Greed

Greed is saying "I will have that entire thing." Greed pushes a person to obtain the item at all cost, even risking one's own survival even though logic says "Don't!" The only logic that exists is "Mine, Mine, Mine" and "See, want, take, have." (Buffy the Vampire Slayer episode Bad Girls)

Greed also doesn't care if someone gets hurt in the process. In fact the Greedy person would call any such harm or loss to others as "Just business." Many of those who end up in prison have hearts of Greed.

Greed's twins are Lust and Gluttony.

## 4. Lust

Lust is saying "I will have that entire person." The person starts thinking that they will have that person even though said person doesn't want anything to do with the Lustful person. If the affections of the Lustful are not noticed or are rejected they get angry and start seeking revenge.

At this point it's all about "If I can't have you no one will." Their vengeance may come as a smear campaign based on lies and rumors or worse. More than one Lustful has gone to prison for rape or murder.

Lust's twins are Greed and Gluttony.

## 5. Gluttony

Gluttony is saying "I will have all of that food." It's more than sitting down at the table and eating way past the point of healthy or socially acceptable. It's about making sure that the food is yours and yours alone and so what if others suffer for doing without. Unlike Greed, Gluttony will not part with food for any amount of money or power, it's all about "Mine."

Gluttony's twins are Greed and Lust.

## 6. Wrath

Wrath is beyond anger. It is beyond hate. It is the Greed for destruction. It is the Lust to inflict pain and suffering. It is the Gluttony for vengeance. Greed is what starts wars and Wrath is what keeps wars going long after the "reason" for it is long gone.

7. <u>Sloth</u>

These days' sloth means being lazy but when this list was originally made it meant Apathy. It meant saying "So what" to the troubles and suffering of others. Now here's the thing, can a person who is donating to charity of any sort still be inflicted with Sloth? How?

In the Gospels there was a point is time where Jesus and his Disciples where watching people go by an offering colocation box. They saw many people rich giving and then they saw a poor person give. Jesus said "this person is going to heaven." Why? Because the others didn't care if their money helped or not while the poor person was giving to try and help others.

# Personalities

❖

In his book <u>New World Order,</u> H.G. Wells says "When I write of Christianity, I mean Christianity with a definite creed and militant organization and not these good kind people." What did he mean by this? When he looked at the Church, what did he see?

Let's start by saying that I've encountered a number of people who sees the Church in the same way as Mr. Wells. They look at the Church, not by looking at Scripture, but looking at the Church's past and current daily actions. What they see is that many of these actions are to control how people act and think. Others actions are meant to keep "others" out of the Church because of their "lack of purity."

Now, the purpose of the Church, according to Scripture, is to provide mutual support to all Christians, to teach the world about who GOD is, and to help bring them closer to understanding HIM. And another purpose of the Church is to render aid to any and all that need it.

To my knowledge, at no point are we given permission from GOD to control anyone or any group of people or any government. And yet, at times, to many believers that seems to be exactly what the Church is about.

At some point in the 80s I started to notice that were different types of Christians. Not Denominations but Personalities. The following are the different Personalities that I have encountered.

*Religious*

Religious Christians won't break GOD's Law but they will bend, twist, and stretch the Law to the point that they can "justify" that their actions are "keeping" the 10 Commandments. These actions include lying, stealing, hating, ignoring, killing, terrorizing, and humiliating "outsiders." They do this by misquoting scripture and/or taking scripture out of context.

To them things like honor, purity, and righteousness is based on how you treat those in the Church and those outside of the church can be treated any old way that one choses.

Their god is their own ego, greed, apathy, and/or hate.

## Legalistic

Legalistic Christians won't break, bend, twist, and/or stretch GOD's Law but they put so much Faith into the Law that the Law becomes their faith not GOD. In effect, what they are doing is giving honor to the pen and paper while ignoring the author. They are worshiping the Law not GOD.

Their god is the Law of Moses but not the GOD of Moses.

## Socialites

Socialite Christians are the "Club-Med" of the Church. To them a "True" Christian wears the Right clothes, drives the Right cars, have the Right jobs, gives to the Right charities, and so on. How they determine what is Right seems to be determined by current fashion mixed in with a little scripture.

To them, if a person "Looks and Acts like a Christian then odiously they are a Christian" without bothering to think that the vilest of sinners can pretend to be a Christian.

Their god is their own vanity.

## Sunday Christians

Sunday Christians are Christians on Sunday but the rest of the week they are sinners. They abuse GOD's willingness to forgive, some to the point that it has no relevance in their hearts.

In truth, their god is their own greed, lust, and gluttony.

## Cattle Christians

Cattle Christians are people who go to church but have neither faith nor reason for going. If you were to ask them "Why do you go to church?" Their answer would be "Well, my parents goes to church, my siblings goes to church, my spouse goes to church, my children goes to church, my co-workers goes to church, and my neighbors goes to church, so I go to church."

Another name for them is Conformist. Conformists don't join a group and behave like the people in the group because they agree with the group but just so they can just fit in. Some do so to make themselves feel complete. Others do so because Human law or tradition requires them to do so.

They have no fire. They are only going through the motions. Revelations 3:15-16 says that HE rejects such people.

In truth, apathy and conformity are their gods.

## True Christians

True Christians don't see the 10 Commandments as a list of things to do. Nor do they see them as tools. When a person becomes a True Christian, the 10 Commandments and the 7 Virtues become descriptions that others use to describe them. How? Because a True Christian LIVES the 10 Commandments and the 7 Virtues; his actions is his testimony, her actions is her witnessing to others, and their actions is their voice to the World proclaiming their beliefs.

If a Christian can be identified by others as a Christian without that person saying a word of scripture or about faith then that person is truly on the Right Path.

A True Christian does most of his testifying with actions and behavior. He is a candle in a dark cave.


## Unknown Believers

Now this one is a bit controversial but as I understand it within the Catholic Faith there is the concept of the Unknown Believer. The idea is that it is possible that someone might know GOD in their heart without knowing HIM in their mind.

Ok, so what does knowing HIM in your mind mean? It means knowing of Him physically. It means knowing the scriptures. It doesn't matter if it's reading the scriptures or hearing the scriptures spoken to you. In other words some level of education about HIM.

So how does one end up as BELIEVER without knowing HIM in your mind? Let's take a look.

The first one is perhaps easy to understand.

The question is what happens to all of the good people who die before a missionary can get to their part of the world and tell them about GOD? Believe it or not but there are those in the Church who say that such people are lost to Hell, period. Personally I find this hard to believe. I have heard of many stories from missionaries about how they tell a group of people about GOD for the first time and someone then tells the missionary "we knew about GOD but we didn't know HIS name."

Also in Matthew 25:34-40 tells of how the Godly People will be rewarded for their actions even though they didn't know the significance of their actions. To me this can very well include those who were never educated about GOD.

In HIS mercy GOD will not hold it against Godly Hearted People for their lack of education.

The second one might be just as easy to understand.

Over the years I have spoken with a number of non-believers about who they think God is. The answers that I get have varied widely but almost all have had one thing in common. Their view of who GOD is, is not based on scripture but on the actions of Church members. They look at us, our beliefs and our actions. But why is it that some of these non-believers turn away from GOD and others towards GOD?

It seems to me that the ones who turn away from GOD are looking at the Church Personalities that I have described as Religious, Legalistic, Socialites, Sunday Christians, and Cattle Christians.

As I have mentioned above these five do not reflect a true image of who GOD is but instead false images. And I it is my firm belief that when they get to the Pearly Gates GOD is going to ask,

"Why did you lead them astray?"

And these people will ask, "Who did we lead astray?"

"These people turned their backs on me and have rejected me. They did so based on you, your beliefs, and your actions. And you beliefs and actions were based not on ME but what you wanted ME to be. You spent your life worshiping a false image of ME that you had created in your mind and heart. And you did so in such a way that others were blinded by your false image and so could not see the real Me. By doing so you have condemned yourself and contributed to their being condemned as well."

Unknown Believers are those who in their heart can see the real GOD even though their mind can only see the false images of GOD.

I believe that God will show mercy on Unknown Believers and allow them into heaven.

# Church Failings

❖

Though divinely lead the Church (like ancient Israel) does not always follow and has fallen and gone astray way too often over the last 2000 years or so. I have noticed that these times seem to fall into different categories.

## *Crusaders*

The 1st Crusade was launched by Pope Urban II in November 1095 and ended with the sack of Jerusalem in July 1099 in which hundreds to possibly thousands of civilians were needlessly killed after the crusaders broke through the city's walls, many of whom were Christians themselves.

On the way to the Holy Lands, many of the crusaders where told by many of the priest, that the only thing they needed to do to be saved was slay the infidels, they need not worry about confession or repentance, just kill the infidels and they will go to Heaven.

This concept was a part of European colonization of the world and part of our American Westward Movement. If you don't believe me ask the Native Americans. It also fueled the many Christian vs. Christian religious wars that has plagued the church through most of its history.

Oddly, if at any time that I've been able to nail down a reason for calling someone an "infidel" the reason is "They are different from us/me."

This concept has been found in all cultures and nations throughout the world and throughout time but the Church and Christians cannot claim it because of Mathew 10:14. "And if the people in a home or a town refuse to listen to you, then leave that place and shake the dust off your feet and leave them to God's mercy."

The thing that I don't get is even though the Crusade concept described above is anti-Biblical why does the Church tolerate it when it should be fighting against it?

## Witch Hunts

The basic concept of the Witch-hunt is that witches always lie which means that the only way to get a truthful confession was through torture. These days it simply means that one is guilty until proven innocent with any and all evidence proving innocence being automatically disregarded. As for who gets accused of being a "witch," it is "that Person is different from me" or "That person disagrees with me." This is often seen in politics and culture here in the US.

The Bible often speaks out against unfair trials, but, like the Crusader concept I described in the above section, the Church most often does not take a stand against this mentality, and when it does the stand, it is often neither long enough nor strong enough to be heard.

## Slavery

In the 19th century much of the Church took a long overdue stand against slavery and won that fight. However, the mentality behind slavery is still around and the Church's stand against it is spotty. The mentality is "Those employees are expendable which means that if they get injured or die so what? They're expendable after all."

Since the end of the American Civil War, the only congregations that take a stand against the Slaver mentality are those tied to a labor union or a civil rights group. The rest at most give lip service to it if any at all.

## Gate Keeper and Keeper of the Keys

The Gate Keeper concept is one where a Church leader(s) says "None shall enter the Church or Heaven without My approval." The standards for getting past these Gate Keepers most often deals little with scripture and more to do with political and cultural bias.

Perhaps the 1st time this mentality entered the Church was when in Acts 15. Some of the early Church Elders said that gentiles should not be allowed in because they weren't following the Law of Moses. What they were really trying say is that "we the Elders can bar the way to those We deem as unclean" forgetting that GOD is open to all.

In the gospels Jesus noted that many of the priesthood did this as well and condemned such actions for it. This makes it very clear that GOD and only GOD is the Gate Keeper and Keeper of the Keys to Heaven.

The Church is often spotty on taking a stand on this issue.

## Divine Right of Kings

This concept is based on the notion that those in charge were put there by GOD and because of this they are infallible and should never ever be questioned or ridiculed nor do they have to follow their own laws. Oddly enough it seems that every time one of the kings of Israel behaved that way GOD would send someone to tell them just how wrong they were. And yet this concept continues to this very day. Many Politicians and CEOs of today act this very way.

I have noticed that more than a few (but not all) leaders of the Church act this way as well.


## Convert or Die

The Bible says that we have two destines and we have freewill to choose between them. The concept of Convert or Die is one where the speaker is saying "Convert to what I believe or I'll punish you." The most common way of enforcing this concept is by outlawing all other beliefs.

The fallacy of this concept is that it is robbing people of their GOD given freewill.


## Like peas in a pod

It is human to categorize people into groups and to judge all in that group by the actions of a few. This tendency is known as stereotyping. This is wrong and dangerous in so many ways.

It is wrong in that one can end up judging you based on the actions of a total stranger. Think about it, how you would like it if someone unfamiliar with Christianity read about the Witch-hunts and then judged you based on the actions of the witch-hunters. Or perhaps as an atheist someone reads about how Stalin, an atheist, killed more than 20 million of his own people and decided that you, because you are an atheist, is just as homicidal as he was.

It is also wrong because you can end up turning a potential friend into an enemy for no reason at all.

Another reason not to do this is that human tendency is to group outsiders together and judging them by the worst of them and ignoring their best. Another tendency is to group insiders together and judging them by the best of them and ignoring the worst. In both cases, what you are doing is lying to yourself about both types of groups and the Bible in so many ways says that lying is a sin.

Also Matthew 7:2 says that as you judge, so you will be judged. To be honest with you I would rather be judged by my actions rather someone else's.

Why the Church is not willing to tackle this one I don't know.


## Intolerance

Jesus showed a lot of tolerance towards believers and nonbelievers of all types and stripes. To me, tolerance is not saying to others, "Go ahead and do what you want." It's explaining to them what you know and believe, it's about answering their questions about what you know, and believe to the best of your ability, and then *allowing* them to make their own decisions. After we do that the only time we should interfere is when they are going to do physical harm to themselves or to others or trying to coerce (take away another's freewill) another into doing wrong.

Too many in the Church seems to confuse "Tolerance" with "Ignoring" or "Endorsing."

# Denominations

These are my thoughts on the various denominations that Christianity has split into over the last 2000 years.

Depending on how one defines a denomination, there are somewhere between 300 and 30,000+ denominations. What separates one from another, can be very minor to extremely major.

I'm of two minds on this. On the one hand, it allows a person to join a congregation that they can be comfortable in. If you enjoy singing, you can join one that does a lot of singing. If you prefer quiet meditation, there is a congregation for you. On the other hand, it can make it very difficult for an outsider to understand what Christianity is and what it means.

From my observations almost all denominations breakdown into three different types.

The first type is cultural. There is a Korean Presbyterian Church here in central Mississippi. The only thing that really separates them from any other Presbyterian Church is that the entire service is done in Korean. To be honest I believe that GOD has no problems with cultural based denominations as long as they are not exclusive. If a non-Korean wanted to join (possibly to improve on their Korean language skills) and the congregation said yes, then they are not being exclusive which is the way HE wants it. However, if they were to say "No, Koreans only," then GOD would have a problem with them.

The second type is theological. An example of this is how to do a baptism. In the Methodist Church, they pour a small amount of water on one's head. In the Baptist Church, the person is placed into a pool of water and then dunked fully into the water. The New Testament says that there is nothing wrong with either method as long as the two don't argue that the other is wrong. This debate did show up in the early Church and ALL of the Apostles told the debaters to shut up and stop arguing over something so minor.

The third type is political. Let's face it, it's very hard for any group of organized persons that is involved in the community to not find itself with some sort of political leanings. However, if the denomination's principles include some form of political statement, then in the end they will stop being a denomination and end up being a political party instead which I feel is not what God wants of us.

# Separation of Church and State

❖

When GOD had Saul anointed as the first king of Israel HE gave some duties to the king and others to the priesthood. One thing that GOD did not do was to give both the same duties. One would think that combining the two would be a good idea and in a perfect world, you would be right. However, we do not live in a perfect world. In looking through history, I have noticed that in governments where religion and state are combined, one of two things always ends up happening.

One, the religion dominates the state. When this ends up happening, the priesthood stops being religious leaders and ends up becoming politicians.

Two, the state dominates the religion. When this ends up happening, the priesthood stops being religious leaders and ends up being servants of the state.

I'm not saying the Church should not have some involvement in government, but to remember to keep a separation between the two. A good example of this would be the Church's involvement in the Civil Rights Movement in the 1950's and 1960's.

# Forgiving Others

What is Forgiveness? What is meant by Forgiving Others?

Over twenty years ago a person hurt me. This person hurt me to the core, took most of what I believed in or enjoyed and mocked them. I wasn't just hurt by this person I was humiliated by this person's treatment of me. I found myself hating this person. I dreamed of this person being knocked down a peg or two, of being hurt, of being torn, of wanting her back into my life. I lived the song "I Miss You" by Blink-182 years before the song was written.

To say that I wanted vengeance is an understatement. I craved it. I hungered for it. I almost prayed for it. Almost.

When I reached that point, I caught myself, seeing the person that I was becoming. I prayed to GOD that I didn't want to be that person, that I didn't want this hate to control me. My prayer was answered. The hate stopped taking me over but it didn't go away. Why? Because I hadn't forgiven her for what she had done.

A couple of weeks after that prayer, I started wanting to forgive her and I prayed about it often, in fact I a prayed at least twice a week about it. About as often, I found the hatred for her rising up in me. After ten years of praying, I finally did what I thought was impossible, I forgave her. When that happened, the hate faded away.

Does this mean that I am willing to take her back into my life? To trust her? No and no.

Forgiving means letting go of one's hate and anger, to give up on one's claim for vengeance on another.

So how often are we to forgive someone?

Matthew 8:22 says "Then Peter came to Jesus and asked 'Lord, when someone won't stop doing wrong to me, how many times must I forgive them? Seven times?' Jesus answered 'I tell you, you must forgive them more than seven times. You must continue to forgive them even if they do wrong to you seventy times seven (70 x 7).'"

Now here's the thing. As I understand, it in ancient times saying "they numbered 40" meant the same today as to say dozens, many, or hundreds, in other words a number beyond count.

So to say 70 x 7 or 490 would in a modern terms mean infinite (∞) times. So God wants us to let go of one's hate and anger, to give up on one's claim for vengeance on someone an infinite number of times.

Ok, why should we? Scripture says that God commands us to forgive others. Ok, so why does He tell us to forgive others? Because Hate is an infection, a wound, it corrupts and makes us do things that can lead up to our own self destruction.

When we are wounded, we have to clean the wound out as soon as possible. If we don't the wound will become infected and infections can cripple or even kill. Before that can happen, we have to clean it out. If you don't clean it out good enough, you'll have to reopen the wound to clean out the infection.

The same is true for emotional and spiritual wounds. If you don't heal these wounds, you can be crippled or even die inside, leaving you hollow. As I have testified, some wounds take time and effort to clean so that healing can begin and to be kept clean so that the healing can be completed. This is what had happened to me.

# Freewill vs.(?) Predestination

❖

The Bible often speaks of prophecy and GOD's ability to see what we are going to do before we even think of doing it. The Bible often speaks of people having the ability to choose their own future, their own destiny. Contradictions yes? Maybe not.

I have read and heard of many scientific experiments to determine if we have freewill or if all of our actions are predetermined by some internal and/or external factors or forces. So far, all experiments that I know of to prove freewill, have proven that we do have freewill. So far all experiments that I know of, to prove predetermination have proven that we do not have freewill at all. Contradictions yes? Maybe not.

The discussions about freewill and predetermination often remind me of the discussions about physics and quantum physics.

In physics, IF you can identify all of the variables of a given object or event AND IF you can give them a correct numerical value AND IF you can come up with an equation that shows how the variables interact with each other AND IF you do your math correctly then YES you can predict the object's or event's future.

In quantum physics, if you know where a given particle is, you have no idea where it is going. If you know where it is going, you have no idea where it is. In short nothing can be predicted about quantum particles.

When you look at the two together, the two should be tearing the universe into shreds. Instead, it seems that in order for one to exist, the other has to exist as well.

How can this be? So far it is unknown how or why.

So it is with freewill and predestination.

It is possible, that if we had freewill without predestination, then all things that could be possible would be possible at the same time at all times. The result would be contradictions and paradoxes at all times and places resulting in a tearing of the universe. If we had predestination without freewill, there would be no changes, no creation or evolution. Death by stagnation would be the fate of the universe.

I'm sure we'll figure it all out at some point once humanity moves on from 1st grade (see **How much do we know?** above).

# Salvation Strings?

The Bible says that Salvation is free and with no strings attached. I have seen more than one non-believer express disbelief saying that there has to be strings attached. I never really understood what they were saying until recently. When I thought about it, yes there are strings attached to salvation. Don't believe me? Let's take a look at these stings;

*String #1*: Admit that one is not perfect. Analogy: Admitting that "yes I am sick."

*String #2*: Admit that while one can handle the symptoms of imperfection, one cannot cure the source of the imperfections. Analogy: Admitting that the cold medicine just ain't cutting it.

*String #3*: GOD is the divine help that is needed to become perfect. Analogy: Time to go see the doctor.

*String #4*: Purge from one's life of the 7 Sins. Analogy: Obey the doctor's orders and take the medicine as told.

*String #5*: LIVE the 10 Commandments and 7 Virtues. Analogy: Listen to the doctor and make those changes in life needed to avoid getting sick again.

*String #6*: Accept the fact that anyone and everyone can receive GOD's grace. Analogy: Accept that the doctor will provide healing to everyone and anyone, even those that you hate.

To be honest, I see these as steps in a process, but I can see how to others they can be strings. But then again, parachutes and suspension bridges are held together by strings so I guess that stings ain't so bad after all.

# Work to be Saved?

There is no work needed to be saved. You have to believe that it is possible and have honest regret over the past wrongs that you have done and truly want to be a different person, a new person, and have faith in God that it can be done.

However, there is often work needed to undo the damage done prior to being saved. Let's take a second look at the "**Salvation String?**" section above.

Everyone who goes to see the doctor is sick, however not all need the same treatment. Some will get "take two and call me in the morning," and others will get "stop eating these foods," and others will get "take these twice a day for the next few months," and a few will get "go home, pack a small bag, and check into this hospital in the morning for further treatment."

Just like in physical healing the spiritual healing needed differs from one person to another and healing often requires work.

# Salvation: Done Deal or Work In Progress?

I heard some preachers say that once you give yourself to GOD, that salvation is a done deal and from that point on you are Heaven bound no matter what happens. I have also heard from other preachers that it is possible to lose your salvation. Both are able to find scripture to support their claims. Personally I believe that they both have a point.

To illustrate this let's use the analogy of a 2-person contract. The contract states what each side is going to give and receive. When GOD puts HIS name on it HE will fulfill HIS end of the contract. As for humans however, we do tend to let things slide, to make errors, and generally fall flat on our face. Yes it is possible for humans to not fulfill our end of the contract.

So for God, it is a done-deal but for humans it is a work-in-progress.

# Testing/Teaching

❖

From time to time the Bible speaks of God testing us. Why would he do so? When the Bible speaks of God as Master it is using the old term which means Teacher and we are His students. There are four reasons why a teacher tests a student.

*Reason #1:* So the teacher can know what the student knows and what he/she can do.

*Reason #2:* So the student can know what he/she knows and what he/she can do.

*Reason #3:* As a way for the teacher to teach the student what he/she knows and what he/she can do.

*Reason #4:* So the student can grow to meet their true potential.

With God He already knows what we know and can do as well as our potential. So it is the other 3 reasons that he tests us.

# 24/7 Prayer?

❖

The Bible in 1 Thessalonians 5:17 says to "Pray without ceasing." What does this mean? Does it mean to give up on sleeping, eating, working, and everything else?

I don't think so. I believe that it means to be in a prayerful state of mind at all times. What that means is to keep your heart, mind, and soul in the state of mind to cleanse the 7 Sins from you, to let the 7 Virtues flow into you, and to keep an open mind to heard GOD speaking to you.

I also believe that we should do the physical act of praying as often as possible so that when we *really need to pray* we can *really pray.*

# Rituals

❖

Call them Rites, Ceremonies, Services, or any similar name, but do they get you into heaven? Legalistic Christians would have you believe that yes they do. What about wearing religious symbols like crosses? Again Legalistic Christians would have you believe that yes they do.

In Matthew 25:31-46 Jesus talks about the end times when we world is gathered together and is then separated into two groups with one going to Heaven and one going to Hell. Among those going to Hell, will be some who will say that they kept the Laws and Rites but GOD will say that HE knows them not.

Ok, so this establishes that the Rites and Symbols themselves won't get you into Heaven, so should they be abandoned or ignored? No, I believe that the purpose of Rites and Symbols are to help you get into the right frame of mind when you worship and pray.

To me they are like survival gear. They help you to survive the environment that you're in like say climbing a mountain. However good the gear is YOU are still the one who has to do the climbing. Just like with Rites and Symbols they can help you but YOU are the one who has to walk the path to Heaven.

This also goes for the argument as to which Rites are the "Correct" Rites. People are different. For some quiet meditation in a group for a couple of hours, works very well. For some listening to a lecture for the same amount of time works. For others singing, dancing, and making a joyful noise to the LORD works just as well. For me, it's siting with a small group of people and talking, discussing, and debating how GOD, the Church, individual believers, and the World relate to each other on any number of topics.

# Views on Hell

❖

There are many different views on what Hell is and what happens to a person should they end up there. There are some who say that being sent there means that you will never leave, others say that after a time it might be possible to leave Hell. Some say that one's punishment is tailored to one's sin, others say that all who go there receive the same punishment.

The view of what Hell is that I wish to address is the one that says that "All who go there will burn in horrible fires for all eternity with no chance of escape." I have found that many, not all, but many say that the punishment of sinners is of extreme importance, that anything different would in one or many ways somehow reduce who GOD is. To them I say "Beware, if your faith in GOD is dependent on the punishment that sinners receive then your faith might not be in GOD but in vengeance which is not the path to heaven."

Do I believe in the existence of Hell? Yes. Do I believe that sinners will receive some form of punishment? Yes. Do I believe that this punishment is eternal? Yes. I also believe that if GOD in His wisdom decides to end a sinner's time and punishment in Hell, then my faith in HIM will not diminish at all, nor will I see HIM becoming less then HE is.

# Obeying His own Laws

❖

I have heard from non-believers that GOD's miracles could not happen because they defy the Laws of Nature.

I have heard from believers that GOD does not have to obey HIS own Laws because HE is GOD. I disagree with both.

First let's look at the non-believers statement. In the Gospels Jesus feeds the 5,000 with only a few loafs of bread and fish. In truth he didn't even need to start with that. According to the Law of Conservation (or Law of Conservation of Information) matter and energy can be neither created nor destroyed but can be changed from one thing or state to another. When you watch a candle burn, you are seeing the candle turn from wax into melted wax (mater), evaporated wax (mater), heat (energy), and light (energy). If you could gather up all of the melted wax, evaporated wax, heat and light and weighed them the total would equal to the weight of the unburnt candle.

Sense it can happen in one direction, the Laws of Nature would most likely allow it to happen in the opposite direction. If this is true, then yes, if you have the right know-how, you can take sunlight and turn it into bread right there in your hands without the "normal" or "scientific" in-between steps. I say that when GOD performed something miraculous HE was using Laws of Nature that we have not learned or even dreamed of as of yet.

Now let's look at the believer's statement. A ruler who cannot or will not follow or obey his own laws is a ruler not worthy of respect or obedience and, since GOD is worthy of both respect and obedience I say, and believe, that HE follows and obeys HIS own laws.

# Fearing God

❖

The Bible says that GOD has the ability to do great destruction. The Bible says to fear GOD for this and that this fear is a positive thing.

I have heard and read many discussions on how this can be true. All are long and winding. Some come close to contradicting themselves. Some do contradict themselves. And most I am unable to understand what they are saying so I have no clue if they are contradicting themselves or not nor do I have any idea if they are correct of not.

So this is what fearing GOD means to me. I fear HIM being disappointed in me. I fear HIM being sad at my actions. I fear failing HIM. Not for the punishments that could follow but for the pain that I had caused HIM.

# Why is there still evil in the World?

❖

This is about as confusing as the "Fearing GOD" discussion above.

The discussions that I have heard and read almost always agree on two points. 1st We have Freewill. 2nd In order for that Freedom to exist there has to be evil.

On the 1st point I agree but I have problem with the 2nd point. The problem is that, before Adam and Eve ate from the Tree of Knowledge of Good and Evil, there was no evil, but there was still Freewill. As I understand Revelations, once all of the End-Times prophecies are fulfilled, Evil will be removed but Freewill will remain.

A 3rd point that is often used is, that GOD is allowing evil and sin to continue is so that for those who fall, they will understand that there are no excuses for their actions.

To my knowledge, the closest the Bible gets to giving us a straight-up answer is in a parable that JESUS gave in Matthew 13:24-29 and 13:36-43;

Matthew 13:24-29

24 Jesus told them another parable: "The kingdom of heaven is like a man who sowed good seed in his field. 25 But while everyone was sleeping, his enemy came and sowed weeds among the wheat, and went away. 26 When the wheat sprouted and formed heads, then the weeds also appeared.

27 "The owner's servants came to him and said, 'Sir, didn't you sow good seed in your field? Where then did the weeds come from?'

28 "'An enemy did this,' he replied.

"The servants asked him, 'Do you want us to go and pull them up?'

29 "'No,' he answered, 'because while you are pulling the weeds, you may uproot the wheat with them. 30 Let both grow together until the harvest. At that time I will tell the harvesters: First collect the weeds and tie them in bundles to be burned; then gather the wheat and bring it into my barn.'"

Matthew 13:36-43

## The Parable of the Weeds Explained

³⁶ Then he left the crowd and went into the house. His disciples came to him and said, "Explain to us the parable of the weeds in the field."

³⁷ He answered, "The one who sowed the good seed is the Son of Man. ³⁸ The field is the world, and the good seed stands for the people of the kingdom. The weeds are the people of the evil one, ³⁹ and the enemy who sows them is the Devil. The harvest is the end of the age, and the harvesters are angels.

⁴⁰ "As the weeds are pulled up and burned in the fire, so it will be at the end of the age. ⁴¹ The Son of Man will send out his angels, and they will weed out of his kingdom everything that causes sin and all who do evil. ⁴² They will throw them into the blazing furnace, where there will be weeping and gnashing of teeth. ⁴³ Then the righteous will shine like the sun in the kingdom of their Father. Whoever has ears, let them hear."

These passages tell me that GOD knows what HE doing.

So what is HE doing? I mean if HE is GOD, so why can't HE just wave HIS hand and make the weeds go away?

As an analogy think of a parent who always picks up after their child and never asks the child to take care of himself. What kind of person will the child turn out to be? A spoiled person is unable to do anything. A wise parent will get the child to do as much as the child can do and takes care of the things that the child is unable to do.

In the same way, if GOD did everything for us what kind people would humanity be? We would be the same as the child. So GOD gets us to do the things that we can do while HE takes care of the things that we cannot.

# Misused and Abused scriptures

There are a number of scriptures that I have noticed that are often used for purposes other than intended. Below are a few.

## Eye for an Eye

Exodus 21:24, Leviticus 24:20, and Deuteronomy 19:21 all speak of Eye-for-an-Eye punishment. Throughout history, many have used Eye-for-an-Eye as justification for vengeance. If they had taken the time to read the verses before and after, they would have learned that the verses are saying that *ALL* PUNISHMENTS *HAS TO BE THE SAME FOR EVERYONE* without regard to race, gender, political beliefs, religious beliefs, class, income, or for any other reasons or excuses; in other words, social equality.

## Vengeance is MINE sayith the LORD

The most common interpretation of Deuteronomy 32:41 is that GOD claims vengeance so that he can be a vengeful god. I believe this to be wrong. Scripture itself supports this. Luke 6:27 says to love your enemies. Vengeance and love are polar opposites, there is no way to do them both.

To understand my interpretation, picture a child playing with something that the child is not supposed to be playing with or playing with it in a wrong or harmful manner. Now picture the parent coming up, taking the item away, saying "this is not yours, it is mine," and then putting it beyond the child's reach so that the child can no longer claim it.

I believe that GOD claims vengeance so that we cannot.

## GOD's *Will be done*

In many places, the Bible speaks of "GOD's WILL be done." This is a testament of having faith in HIM even when the world or even logic itself seems to be breaking down. However, way to many times, I have seen it misused and abused.

At times I have seen it used as a dismissive, a way of saying "oh well" or "I care not." I have also seen it as a way of saying "rotten luck" or "sucks to be you."

The worst use is to use it as an excuse for one's actions such as lying, theft, or murder.

# Morality

❖

One of the things that I have seen is the slow eroding of morality in some of those who are supposed to be the Church's Guardians. To me, the first sign of this is saying that "Morality is hindering us" or "Morality is secondary" or "Morality is to be used amongst Us but not necessarily on Them." When one of these phrases, or variation thereof, is spoken, that person has taken the first step on a long and dark road that can only lead to hell on earth and Hell itself for the speaker. Once that step has been taken, inevitably one of two things will happen; either the person will step away from this path or will take the next step.

After that first step is taken, the next step on this path is "The Ends justifies the Means." At this point, it simply means overlooking or not mentioning small things that might not help in reaching the Ends. This step is where most people tend to stop. However, the temptation to continue on is strong. For some it is too strong. Again once that step has been taken, inevitably one of two things will happen; either the person will turn away from this path or will take the next step.

The second step is a continuation of "The Ends justifies the Means." This step is defined by lying by omission, the flat out leaving out of facts and information. It is also defined by strong denial and stronger redirection back onto the other person's flaws. This is not a constructive pointing out of a person failings and faults to help the person but as a form of attack. Unfortunately I myself once or twice have stood at this point and this is a sin that I repent of and seek to not repeat. And yet again once that step has been taken, inevitably one of two things will happen; either the person will walk away from this path or will take the next step.

The third step is another continuation of "The Ends justifies the Means." This is not just lying but the outright misrepresentation of not just facts and information but of the World itself. These people assume that all who listen are automatically accepting and believing what this person is saying and gets offended or even angry when the listener questions even the smallest part of what the speaker has said. And yet again once that step has been taken, inevitably one of two things will happen; either the person will repent and turn away from this path or will take the next step.

The forth step is the culmination of "The Ends justifies the Means." By this time, Arrogance and Hate are in control of the person. If you are not a follower of this person, you are an enemy of this person and EVERYTHING is Legal, Good, Pure, and Holy as long as it is used to destroy you. This person sees himself/herself as purifying the earth and storming the Gates of Hell itself. But the truth is that they have brought hell to earth and is entering Hell as one of its inmates.

# Some Closing Thoughts

❖

While we are called upon to save people's souls we must be careful not to condemn them in the process. The 1st reason is because it is not our place to do so. The 2nd reason is until we can pull out the logs of our eyes (i.e. Church faults and our wayward brethren as well as any personal faults) we are not able to point out the splinters in the eyes of others.

This is very important because if we were to somehow provide absolute proof to science that GOD is indeed real without clearing up the faults within the Church and without getting our wayward brethren within our ranks back on the right path then nonbelievers could end up fearing GOD for the wrong reasons. They could see HIM as an enemy and the fault for this would fall on us.

Printed in the United States
By Bookmasters